Grammar
Puzzles & Mazes

By Jim Halverson

Grades 4–8

SCHOLASTIC
PROFESSIONAL BOOKS

New York • Toronto • London • Auckland • Sydney
Mexico City • New Delhi • Hong Kong • Buenos Aires

Julia Cummings

Dedication

My colleagues at Saint Ann's School asked for and inspired this book and its two companions, my students (no-nonsense editors!) enthusiastically helped me revise all three, and my family, dear Anita and Leif, supported and encouraged and often suffered through the writing process over several long years.

Cover design by Kelli Thompson
Interior design by Grafica, Inc.
Interior illustrations by Dave Clegg

ISBN 0-439-05186-X

Table of Contents

Introduction

What This Book Is...

he exercises in this book rest upon two assumptions: that students learn best when they are having fun, and that most students need frequent repetition of grammar concepts in order to retain them. These units are designed to help you address both needs. Instead of another grammar quiz to test and demonstrate their knowledge, students get to solve a puzzle, complete a maze, or figure out what is wrong with a picture.

The exercises are also designed to suit a range of instructional needs. They can be used as part of a whole-class lesson or for individual enrichment, and they meet a range of skill levels. The units have two or three separate exercises, each a bit harder and more sophisticated than the one before. You may find that only one of the exercises in a given unit is appropriate for the age or skill level of the students you teach, or you may wish to work your way up through all of them.

...And Is Not

The introduction to each unit provides helpful definitions, grammar rules, examples, and a mini-lesson. However, these introductions are not designed to be complete teaching guides. Similarly, the exercises are meant to supplement and enrich your teaching, not to provide a complete or methodical program for each concept. For easier grammatical concepts, you may find that the exercises here provide sufficient practice for students, but for stubborn problems, such as agreement errors and the difference between *lie* and *lay*, you are surely going to want to build up to these exercises with preliminary work. You may want to use these puzzles and mazes as enjoyable rewards for mastering those tough concepts.

Before You Start...

Since the exercises require that students have a working knowledge of the grammar concepts involved, it is very important for you to familiar-ize yourself with a unit before using it. Make sure that you have covered all the decisions that your students will have to make when they tackle the activity. Within the unit, check the degree of difficulty of the exercises and decide which pages best suit your students. Generally, the first page is probably best for fourth, fifth, and sixth grades, and the second and third pages are best for sixth, seventh, and eighth grades, but these can be only very rough guidelines since classes vary so greatly. Several units that deal with difficult concepts, like dangling participles, are intended for older or more sophisticated students; similarly, the review units at the end require a thorough knowledge of a variety of concepts.

...And After You Finish

I hope that you will connect the grammar activity pages in this book to real-world writing and help students see that an understanding of grammar and usage is really just a small part of a bigger picture—written communication. The sooner they can apply a grammatical concept to their own writing, the sooner that concept will be theirs for life. For instance, after the students work on exercises from the units on agreement, you might give a writing assignment which asks them to use several constructions involving singular indefinite pronouns, like *each*, *either*, *neither*, and *anyone*. Or after they complete the irregular verb exercises, you might have your younger students proofread their own writing for verb errors by pretending that they are detectives looking for mistakes that a "bad-usage" suspect may have made.

Finally, don't forget that knowledge of standard usage is just one of many writing skills and not an end in itself. Some of your students—some of us!—are going to continue to use *like* in non-standard ways and to make occasional agreement errors, but those lapses should not prevent them from writing well. A working knowledge of grammar can help your students become successful writers who communicate freshly, vividly, forcefully, and delightfully. —Jim Halverson

Unit 1: Basic Subject-Verb Agreement

Phrases after the subject often causes agreement errors. There are also often problems in sentences beginning with *here*, *there*, and *where*.

This unit covers the agreement of subject and verb in *number*, i.e., whether a noun or verb is *singular* (representing one) or *plural* (representing more than one).

Rule: If the subject of a sentence is singular in number, then the verb must be singular; if the subject is plural, the verb must be plural.

Example: This *box is* empty . . .   but these *boxes are* full.
(singular subject and verb)   (plural subject and verb)

Teaching Tips

★ When a phrase comes between the subject and verb, we can be fooled by the additional nouns or pronouns closer to the verb: This *box* of roofing nails *are* missing. Of course the verb in this last sentence should be *is* because the subject of the sentence is *box*, not *nails*.

★ Sentences that begin with *here*, *there*, and *where* also can be troublesome because in speech we so often contract these words to *here's*, *there's*, and *where's*: *Here's my mother and father* instead of *Here are my mother and father*.

★ A tricky coincidence is that English verbs in the third person singular of the present tense end in s just like plural nouns: one dog barks; two dogs bark. As a result, students who know that the subject is plural sometimes mistakenly use the verb form that ends in s (two dogs barks), thinking that the s must make the words agree.

Mini-Lesson

Students make frequent agreement errors because they so often hear incorrect usage, even from supposedly educated speakers, like newscasters. I recently heard a reporter say, "Now there's two fires raging on that same block!" A good way to introduce this unit, then, is to do a short oral drill to give your students practice hearing standard subject and verb agreement.

Review the agreement rule above and point out the frequent causes of agreement errors—intervening phrases and sentences that start with *here*, *there*, and *where*. Then tell your students that you are going to read some sentences aloud, and they must tell you whether the sentence is correct or contains an agreement error. Have a list of about twenty sentences ready to read, making sure that you concentrate on frequent errors like *There's two fires raging* and *The clothes in the dryer is still not ready*.

Answers

Page 7, What Is Wrong Here?
Changes needed: Signs: ...Flowers Are...; ...Citizens Don't... **Book title:** ...Dog Doesn't... **Picnickers:** ...bees seem...; Aren't there... slices...?; ...bag...has.... **Kids and dog:** ...Skippy...loves....; boy and girl...get...! **Kids and rose:** ...father and mother raise...; thorns...look...! **Squirrel:** ...haven't...humans...? **Birds:** ...beaches and parks provide....

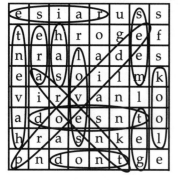

Page 8, Solve the Riddle
1. Does **2.** have **3.** aren't **4.** are (no error) **5.** were **6.** are **7.** doesn't **8.** hasn't (no error) **9.** sell **10.** have **11.** want **12.** hopes
Answer to riddle: an envelope

Page 9, Maze
The correct path goes through: 1. Here is my car! **2.** My pen doesn't work. **3.** That shirt with no buttons looks odd. **4.** Have the dogs in this pen been fed? **5.** Your directions to the movie theater were very easy to follow. **6.** The results of the election are already posted. **7.** My pants and shirt match well. **8.** Doesn't that boy look like my cousin? **9.** The price of most of the products in these stores is too high. **10.** Three of the teachers in my school sing in my church choir. **11.** The time for fun and games has come! **12.** The winner of both games was Tai. (Go through the "secret passage.") **13.** Have the people in back gone out yet? **14.** Here's the way! **15.** The result of your efforts is real success. **Bonus:** There are 18 correct sentences in all.

Grammar Puzzles & Mazes • Scholastic Professional Books

Name _____ Date _____

What Is Wrong Here?

Agreeable Park is a favorite spot for wildlife, but if you look carefully you'll see that some of the people and even the animals don't make their subjects and verbs agree very well.

Directions: Find and correct 12 agreement errors in the picture. Locate the correct verb forms in the word find in the middle of the picture.

Mom, my bag of potato chips have ants in it.

Why do the insects enjoy my picnics more than my kids do?

Isn't there any more slices of ham?

The bees seems to like my soda, too.

In July beaches and parks provides good people-watching opportunities.

Look! There is a rare red-crested, freckle-faced boy!

Why hasn't these humans brought any nuts?

Are you exercising enough?

My father and mother raises roses.

The thorns on that rose looks dangerous!

e	s	i	a	r	u	s	s
t	e	h	r	o	g	e	f
n	r	a	l	a	d	e	s
e	a	s	o	i	l	m	k
v	i	r	v	a	n	l	o
a	d	o	e	s	n	t	o
h	r	a	s	n	k	e	l
p	n	d	o	n	t	g	e

Sometimes he catches it in the air.

That boy and girl of mine just never gets tired of this silly game!

Good Citizens Doesn't Litter

Skippy just love to fetch the ball!

Don't Pick: The Flowers Is for Everyone!

A Trained Dog Don't Bite

Name _____   **Date** _____

Solve the Riddle

I start with the letter *e*,
I end with the letter *e*.
I contain only one letter,
Yet I am not the letter *e*!
What am I?

Directions: To find the answer to the riddle, correct the subject and verb agreement problems in the sentences below. If there is a mistake, write the correct form of the verb in the spaces that follow the sentence. Write the letter that you have placed over any numbered space in the matching answer space. (Leave the spaces blank after correct sentences.) The first one has been done for you.

Answer: __ __   __ __ __ __ __ __ __ $\frac{e}{10}$
          1 2   3 4 5 6 7 8 9

1. *Does*
   ~~Do~~ your shirt need to be washed? $\underline{d}\ \underline{o}\ \underline{e}\ \underline{s}$
                                              10

2. The counselors at camp all has their own first aid kits.   __ __ __ __
                                                                      3

3. There isn't enough apples for a pie.   __ __ __ __ ' __
                                                   2

4. Your ideas about the school fair are really helpful.   __ __
                                                           9

5. The members of the union was planning to strike.   __ __ __ __
                                                            6

6. Where is your new shoes?   __ __ __
                              1

7. The box of chocolates don't weigh very much.   __ __ __ __ ' __
                                                        8

8. Hasn't the paint on the banisters dried yet?   __ __ __ __ __ __ ' __
                                                        2

9. My aunt and uncle often sells things in yard sales.   __ __ __ __
                                                                7

10. What has all those people done with their luggage?   __ __ __ __
                                                                5

11. Nan and Lori really wants you on their team.   __ __ __ __
                                                          4

12. The leader of the committee hope the bill will pass.   __ __ __ __
                                                                  9

READY-TO-GO REPRODUCIBLES

Punctuation Puzzles & Mazes • Scholastic Professional Books

Name _____ **Date** _____

Maze

Directions: Find the path to the end by passing only through areas that have sentences in which the subject and verb agree. Be careful! There are false paths and one sneaky "secret passage." The correct path will take you through 15 correct sentences.

☀ **Bonus:** How many correct sentences are in the entire maze? ____

START

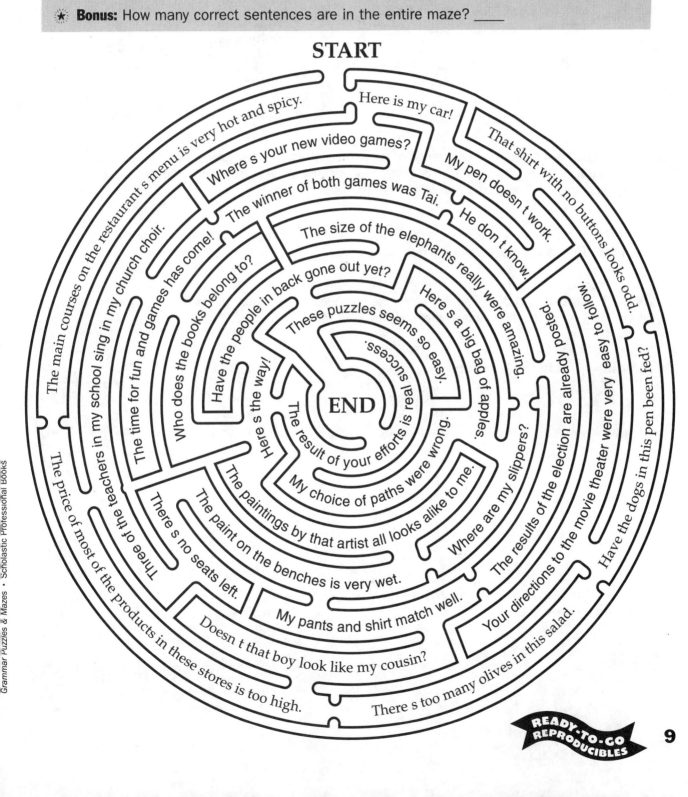

Unit 2: Subject-Verb Agreement: Indefinite Pronouns and Compound Subjects

> Each of the singular indefinite pronouns, like *each* and *anyone*, cause frequent errors.

This unit builds on students' knowledge of basic subject and verb agreement and introduces them to the harder problems caused by *indefinite pronouns* (like *each* and *nobody*) and by *singular compound subjects* connected with *or* and *nor* (like *Alex or Alicia*).

Definition: *Indefinite pronouns* are common third-person pronouns that don't refer to particular subjects. They are grouped below by number.

Rule 1: If the subject of a sentence is a singular indefinite pronoun, the verb must be singular; if the subject is a plural indefinite pronoun, the verb must be plural.

Singular Indefinite Pronouns			Examples
each	one	anyone	**Each** of the boys *is* here.
everyone	someone	no one	*Does* **anybody** know her?
nobody	anybody	everybody	**Neither** of them *likes* the book.
somebody	either	neither	

Plural Indefinite Pronouns			Examples
both	few	many	**Both** of them *like* the book.
several			*Do* **many** of you know her?

Singular or Plural Indefinite Pronouns *(Depending on Context)*			Examples
all	any	most	**All** of the boys *are* here.
some	none		**All** of the money *is* here.
			Do **most** of the chapters amuse you?
			Does **most** of the book amuse you?

READY-TO-GO REPRODUCIBLES

Grammar Puzzles & Mazes • Scholastic Professional Books

Teaching Tip

★ *None* used to be among the words in the singular list, and some writers still use it only in a singular sense: *None of the students* was *absent.* Most writers would now, however, express this idea: *None of the students* were *absent* or *Not one of the students* was *absent.*

Rule 2: Compound subjects that are singular and are connected by *or* or *nor* require a singular verb; if both subjects in the compound are plural, the verb is plural.

Examples: Either **he or she** *is* mistaken.

Neither **Frieda nor her sister** *was* there.

Neither **the boys nor the girls** *are* ready.

Teaching Tip

★ Sentences with *or* or *nor* connecting one singular and one plural subject should probably be rewritten. Some experts, however, say that it is acceptable to make the verb agree with the closer subject: *Neither **Frieda nor** the other **girls** were there.*

Mini-Lesson

Indefinite pronouns and the *or* and *nor* conjunctions cause such frequent agreement mistakes in conversation that students are likely to think that the mistakes they hear are actually correct. For example, it's difficult to hear what's wrong in the sentence *Each of the students need help.*

Explain to your students that the agreement of verbs and indefinite pronouns that are always plural usually doesn't give people trouble. Let them compare a few examples, such as *All of the students need help* and the nonstandard *All of the students needs help.*

Thus they will need to watch out for only the *singular* indefinite pronouns. To make their memorization task much easier, point out that many of these words show us they're singular—they include the suffix *-one* or *–body*. And the words that use neither suffix can be thought of as referring to *one* thing (*neither one* or *each one*).

Answers

Page 12, Maze
The correct path goes through: 1. Is each of the birds this tall? **2.** Not one of them is moving! **3.** Both Nan and Carol have seen pelicans here. **4.** Everyone in my group has finished sketching them. **5.** One of the biggest flamingos is about to fly! **6.** Flamingos are such regal birds! **7.** Nobody is ready to go home yet. **8.** There's the ranger. **9.** Is every one of their feathers pink? **10.** Neither of my parents has ever seen one.

Pages 13–14, Hidden Message
1. has **2.** Does **3.** is, are **4.** Has, does **5.** wants **6.** Where are **7.** Does **8.** are, feels **9.** come, looks **10.** Has **11.** has **12.** is, seem
Answer: Yes; 91

Page 15, Puzzle
1. Has **2.** was **3.** have **4.** has **5.** Where are **6.** Does **7.** gets, want **8.** are **9.** knows, get **10.** puts **11.** There are, makes **12.** has
Puzzle answer: mash the potatoes

Subject-Verb Agreement: Indefinite Pronouns and Compound Subjects

Name _____ **Date** _____

Maze

Directions: Find the path from start (**S**) to finish (**F**) by passing only through areas that have sentences with correct subject-verb agreement. The correct path will take you through 10 correct sentences.

There's at least a hundred flamingos near that little lake.

Neither of my parents has ever seen one.

Everybody here seem so excited!

Nobody is ready to go home yet.

Flamingos are such regal birds!

Everyone in my group has finished sketching them.

Do Ruth or Toni have any more snacks for us?

Several birds in the water is fishing.

One of the biggest flamingos is about to fly!

There's the ranger.

Neither Bo nor Lori were able to come.

Each of the students has a bird guide.

Both Nan and Carol have seen pelicans here.

Where's all the binoculars?

Is every one of their feathers pink?

Not one of them is moving!

Neither she nor Jana were feeding them.

Is each of the birds this tall?

S

READY-TO-GO REPRODUCIBLES

Name _____   **Date** _____

Hidden Message

Angela was sure she had done well on Mr. Marcos's data and graphing test. She estimated she'd earned an A-. Was she right? Complete the exercise below to reveal her score in the graph on the chalkboard.

Directions: In each sentence, underline the correct form of the verb. Then shade the square in the chalkboard graph that matches the letter-number pair above your answer. When you have shaded in all the correct squares, Angela's score will appear on the graph. The first one has been done for you.

Name _____ **Date** _____

Hidden Message (continued)

1. One of my best friends (have, <u>has</u>) three cats and two dogs.
   ^{A7   D3}

2. (Do, Does) this bus go all the way to the Monster Mall?
   ^{E1   F6}

3. There (is, are) not enough meat in my sandwich, and both pieces of bread (is, are) stale.
   ^{B2   C5}   ^{B8   F2}

4. (Have, Has) each of the students brought paper and (do, does) every one of them have art supplies?
   ^{C3   C6}   ^{A5   B4}

5. Neither Julia nor Nicole (wants, want) to see that movie.
   ^{D4   F8}

6. (Where's, Where are) my hat and gloves?
   ^{G4   E6}

7. (Do, Does) anybody here remember the school telephone number?
   ^{E2   C2}

8. Charlene and James (is, are) both applying for summer jobs, but neither of them (feel, feels) too confident about getting one.
   ^{C8   B3}   ^{B5   C4}

9. Here (come, comes) all of the campers, and every one of them (looks, look) tired.
   ^{G3   B1}   ^{B6   E5}

10. (Have, Has) either you or Ramon had chicken pox?
    ^{A3   D6}

11. Every one of my cousins (has, have) sent birthday greetings.
    ^{D2   B7}

12. Either of the two main courses (are, is) fine, but both of them (seem, seems) a little expensive.
    ^{F7   E4}   ^{F4   D5}

Grammar Puzzles & Mazes • Scholastic Professional Books

READY-TO-GO REPRODUCIBLES

Name _____ **Date** _____

Puzzle

A mother has six children and three potatoes. How can she feed each an equal amount without cutting the potatoes in half or using fractions?

Answer: __ __ __ __   __ __ __   __ __ __ __ __ __ __ <u>s</u>
1 2 3 4   5 6 7   8 9 10 11 12 13 14 15

Directions: To find the answer to the puzzle, circle the correct verb forms in the sentences below. For each circled answer, write the underlined letter in the matching answer space above. The first one has been done for you.

1. (H⁶a<u>ve</u>, (H¹⁵a<u>s</u>)) everyone finished eating?

2. The height of the redwood trees (w¹¹a<u>s</u>, we²<u>re</u>) hard to determine.

3. Both Teddy and Annette (ha⁴<u>s</u>, ⁶<u>h</u>ave) brought extra snacks.

4. Neither of the beds (ha³<u>s</u>, hav⁹<u>e</u>) any sheets or blankets.

5. (Where'⁸<u>s</u>, Where ar¹⁴<u>e</u>) all the pencils and pads?

6. (⁶<u>D</u>o, D⁹<u>o</u>es) every one of the rakes have a broken handle?

7. Neither Jacqueline nor Cindy (ge⁵<u>t</u>s, ¹³<u>g</u>et) seasick, and both of them (wa¹<u>n</u>ts, wan¹²<u>t</u>) to go on the cruise.

8. Several of the students in my art class (¹⁰<u>i</u>s, ar⁷<u>e</u>) firing pots in the kiln.

9. Each of the girls on the basketball team (kn¹³<u>o</u>ws, kno⁸<u>w</u>) the plays well, but not all of them (g²<u>e</u>ts, ge¹⁰<u>t</u>) to play in every game.

10. Neither Cassie nor her friend Tessa (⁸<u>p</u>uts, pu²<u>t</u>) mustard on hot dogs.

11. (There'¹<u>s</u>, There ²a<u>re</u>) lots of different flowers in that bouquet, and every one of them (¹<u>m</u>akes, ma⁴<u>k</u>e) me sneeze.

12. Either he or she (⁴<u>h</u>as, hav⁴<u>e</u>) made a mistake.

READY-TO-GO REPRODUCIBLES

Unit 3: Pronoun-Antecedent Agreement

One of the pronouns didn't agree with their antecedent.

its

This unit concentrates on problems involving the agreement in number between a pronoun and its antecedent.

Definition: An antecedent is the noun or pronoun to which a pronoun refers.

Rule: If the antecedent of a pronoun is singular, the pronoun must be singular; if the antecedent of a pronoun is plural, the pronoun must be plural.

> **Examples:** The *maze* was confusing. **It** twisted and turned unexpectedly. (*Maze* is the antecedent of **It**.)
>
> *Each* of the boys found **his** (not **their**) own way. (The antecedent of **his** is *each*, not *boys*.)
>
> *Neither* of the women in the play had studied **her** lines. (*Neither*, not *women*, is the antecedent of **her**.)

Teaching Tips

★ The *singular indefinite pronouns* (see page 10 for a list) give students the most trouble with pronoun agreement, especially when they are followed by a phrase ending in a plural noun, as in the second and third examples above.

★ Longer sentences with many words between the pronoun and its singular noun antecedent also frequently cause problems.

> **Example:** If a *woman* has constant aches and pains and has trouble sleeping most nights, then maybe **she** (not **they**) should consult a doctor.

READY-TO-GO REPRODUCIBLES

Grammar Puzzles & Mazes • Scholastic Professional Books

★ The problem of indefinite pronoun agreement is exacerbated by the fact that pronouns must agree with their antecedents in gender as well as number.

Example: If *anyone* calls, tell _____ I'll be right back.

We have three pronoun options here:

1. We can use the historically correct but sometimes sexist pronoun *him* or the exclusionary *her*.

2. We can use the awkward combination *him or her*.

3. We can use the nonstandard plural *them*.

In writing it is usually best to avoid the problem altogether by changing the antecedent to a plural form (*If* people *call, tell* them *I'll be right back*) or recasting the sentence entirely (*Tell anyone who calls that I'll be right back*).

Mini-Lesson

Since we all constantly hear—and use—incorrect pronoun agreement in informal speech to avoid the problem of gender agreement, it is extremely difficult for students to recognize (or often even to accept) standard agreement. An oral drill can help them get used to hearing standard forms.

First, go over the reasons (outlined above) that we often choose nonstandard plural forms when we talk, and then discuss the appropriateness of using informal English when we talk with friends but standard English when we write. Next, let students hear the standard usage in clear and easy sentences like *Did either of the boys forget his homework?* Finally, on the board write a list of amusing sentences with the problem pronouns missing and call on students to correctly fill in the blanks.

Examples: Neither Jody nor Cheryl had remembered to tell _____ boyfriend about the party. Every one of the snakes escaped from _____ cage.

Answers

Pages 18–19, What Are They?
Correct sentences: 1, 3, 6, 7, 9, 11, 14, 15
Corrections for incorrect sentences:
2. Neither Roland nor Manuel...with *him*.
4. Does Quincy or Cody...*his* set? **5.** Is everybody...*her* projects? **8.** If you see a character...*he* (or *she*) often seems... **10.** When a TV reporter...*he* (or *she*) tries... **12.** Anyone...*his* (or *her*) parents' permission... **13.** One...had *his* back turned...
Mystery Object 1: (circled clues) ice cream cone **Mystery Object 2:** (underlined clues) hot dog

Page 20, Maze
The correct path goes through: 1. One of the lobsters... **2.** Neither of the explorers...
3. Each of the sleds... **4.** Neither of the fishing... **5.** Several of the Canada... **6.** Every one of the cowboys... **7.** Neither of the girls...

Page 21, Number Puzzle
Correct sentences: 3, 6, 10, 12 **Corrected sentences (number of errors in parentheses):**
1. Should everybody...*his* (or *her*) coins... (1)
2. Neither...in *his* coin collection. (1) **4.** Did either...silver in *it*? (1) **5.** One...on *its* back, which means *it* came... (2) **7.** Neither...*he* wanted...*his* coins. (2) **8.** Every one...that *she* would...*her* help. (2) **9.** If one...*his* change... tell *him*... (2) **11.** Every one...*he* often found...*he* walked *his* beat. (3) **13.** Every one...*its* date... (1) **14.** If a person...*he* (or *she*) can count... (1)
Puzzle answer: 16 coins total (9 quarters, 1 dime, 2 nickels, and 4 pennies)

Pronoun-Antecedent Agreement

Name _____ **Date** _____

What Are They?

Directions: Sort out the mixed-up clues in the Clue Box to discover two mystery objects. First, identify the sentences on page 19 in which the pronouns and antecedents agree and those in which they do not. When you find a correct sentence, (circle) the clue number that follows the sentence. When you find an incorrect sentence, make the correction and underline the clue number that follows the sentence. Use the circled clues to identify the first object and use the underlined clues to identify the second object.

Mystery Object 1: _____
(circled clues)

Mystery Object 2: _____
(underlined clues)

CLUE BOX

Clue 1: Most people want it warm, and some make it spicy.

Clue 2: It is usually about as long as a new pencil.

Clue 3: It goes from tiny to about the width of a doorknob.

Clue 4: Turn it upside down, and it looks like someone wearing a tall hat.

Clue 5: Europeans created the basics, but Americans made it into this.

Clue 6: Its name contains three c's and three e's.

Clue 7: Its name does not, happily, tell what it's really made of.

Clue 8: The last word in its name describes a shape and rhymes with *zone*.

Clue 9: It is cold and sticky.

Clue 10: The first word of its name is nice, but only if you add a letter.

Clue 11: Its name contains two words, each with an *o*.

Clue 12: To write it you need three words.

Clue 13: The last word of its name rhymes with *hog*.

Clue 14: You often find these at baseball games.

Clue 15: If you don't eat it quickly, it may run away.

READY·TO·GO REPRODUCIBLES

Grammar Puzzles & Mazes • Scholastic Professional Books

What Are They? (continued)

1. The teacher gave every one of the girls in the gym class her own personal exercises. (Clue 3)

2. Neither Roland nor Manuel had baseball gloves with them. (Clue 2)

3. Each of these submissions to the magazine must be sent in its own envelope. (Clue 12)

4. Does Quincy or Cody have a favorite song selected for their set? (Clue 1)

5. Is everybody on the Women's Action Committee here and ready with their projects? (Clue 11)

6. If a football player is going to play a full game, he must be in very good shape. (Clue 6)

7. Neither of the girls thought that she had dressed appropriately for the party. (Clue 15)

8. If you see a character in a movie whom you've met first in a book, they often seem strange and disappointing. (Clue 14)

9. Every single car in his shop had had its bumper crushed in the same accident. (Clue 4)

10. When a TV reporter interviews you, they try to make you relax and "be natural." (Clue 7)

11. Did either of the dogs hurt itself on the broken glass? (Clue 10)

12. Anyone who fails to get their parents' permission will not be allowed to go to the zoo. (Clue 5)

13. One of the two men in the photograph had their back turned to the camera. (Clue 13)

14. Neither Pauline nor Marcella had her mind on her work. (Clue 9)

15. Each of the stories in the book had its own surprising plot twists. (Clue 8)

Maze

Name _____

Date _____

Directions: Find the path across Canada from start (**S**—in New Brunswick) to finish (**F**—on Vancouver Island) by passing only through areas that have sentences in which pronouns agree. You may go overland from province to province or use a boat or airplane where there are paths indicated by dotted lines. The correct path to the finish will take you through seven correct sentences.

- - - - - = Boat or airplane trip

╪ or ╤ or ╫ = Border crossing

Name _____ **Date** _____

Number Puzzle

Jacqueline decided to buy a new pen that cost $2.49. She had exact change and she paid with the fewest possible coins, using at least one quarter, one dime, one nickel, and one penny. How many coins did she use? How many of each coin did she use?

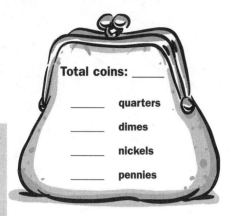

Total coins: _____

_____ quarters

_____ dimes

_____ nickels

_____ pennies

Directions: Find the total number of pronoun and antecedent agreement errors in each sentence below. Make your corrections and write in the number of errors on the line next to each sentence. When you've finished, tally up the number of corrections you've made to find out how many coins Jacqueline used.

___ **1.** Should everybody bring their coins to the first coin collector's meeting?

___ **2.** Neither of my brothers ever had a buffalo nickel in their collection.

___ **3.** Not one of the silver dollars had its value set at less than $100.

___ **4.** Did either the Roosevelt dime or the Mercury dime have much silver in them?

___ **5.** One of my dimes had a tiny letter s on their back, which means that they came from the San Francisco mint.

___ **6.** Each of the two nickels had Jefferson's picture on its front and Monticello, Jefferson's home, on its back.

___ **7.** Neither of the teachers thought that they wanted to display their gold coins.

___ **8.** Every one of the girls in Mrs. Anderson's class said that they would give us their help at Club Night.

___ **9.** If one of your fathers saves their change in a jar, tell them I'd like to look through it for valuable coins.

___ **10.** Does either the Liberty dollar or the Susan B. Anthony dollar contain real silver?

___ **11.** Every one of the policemen whom I spoke to said that they often found coins when they walked their beat.

___ **12.** If each of the girls would contribute one hour of her time, then we could get the gym set up for the coin show.

___ **13.** Every one of the Indian Head pennies had been in circulation so long that their date had worn off.

___ **14.** If a person has lots of very old coins, they can count on some of them being valuable.

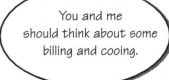

Unit 4: Pronoun Case

You and me should think about some billing and cooing.

In CASE you don't know, my nestmate and I are falcons, and we raptors feast on birds with bad usage.

The exercises in this unit deal with the problems that students sometimes have choosing the correct personal pronouns in sentences that use compound subjects (*She and I*) and *objects (me and them)*.

Definition: Personal pronouns—*I*, *we*, *she*, *her*, *they*, *them*, and so on—stand in for people or things and so have to show whether they *do* the action of the sentence (subjects) or have the action *done to them* (objects). Words show us their use by their form, or *case*—*I* and *me*, for instance, refer to the same person, but *I* performs an action (*I* is a subject), and *me* is acted upon (*me* is an object).

Rule: The agents of the action in a sentence should be in the **subjective case**; the recipients of the action should be in the **objective case**.

> **Examples:** Ben and *I* bought tickets for **them**.
>
> *They* bought tickets for Ben and **me**.
>
> *We* paid for **them**; *they* paid for **us**.

Teaching Tips

★ Compound subjects or compound objects often give students trouble. Here's a typical error: *Miranda and* me *gave the tickets to Lily and* she. For some reason the use of a noun with the pronoun makes it much harder to hear the case errors in that sentence; almost no one would make a mistake if those nouns weren't there:

Grammar Puzzles & Mazes • Scholastic Professional Books

Me *gave the tickets to* she?
Of course not: I *gave the tickets to* her.
Thus: *Miranda and* I *gave the tickets to Lily and* her.

Trying out the pronouns by themselves in that way—temporarily making the subject simple instead of compound—is a great way to see if pronouns are being used correctly.

★ The same technique can be used for a pronoun linked with a defining noun: *Give the tickets to* we *boys.* Try the sentence without the noun:

Give the tickets to we?
No. *Give the tickets to* us.
Thus: *Give the tickets to* us *boys.*

Mini-Lesson

The key to avoiding case errors is to recognize the situations when they are likely to occur, namely when personal pronouns are used in compound constructions (as in the example featuring Miranda and Lily) or when they are used with a defining noun (*Give the tickets to us boys*). A good way to help students remember these situations is, in essence, to work backwards by having them create sentences in which a case mistake might be hard to detect.

First, show your students a sample sentence with a single pronoun subject: *At lunch we saw Maria.* Now say that you are going to add some words and try to sneak in a case error or two that someone might not hear: *At lunch us girls saw Maria and he.* Finally, ask them each to create a few sentences that try to "sneak in" some case errors. These example sentences can be shared orally as a fun drill. Challenge students to test the sentences by isolating the personal pronouns in the compound subject and compound object. (In the above example, they would eliminate *girls* and *Maria and*; the resulting *At lunch us saw he* would then be corrected to *At lunch we saw him*.) By working backwards, students learn how to manipulate personal pronouns in subject and object cases.

Answers

Page 24, Treasure Hunt
The correct clues are: 1. Rachelle, if you and she look where Dad and I grow vegetables, you will find <u>a</u>nother clue. **2.** Go to <u>t</u>he place where the neighbors and we share a gate. **3.** It's up to you and her to find the <u>r</u>ight clue where you and I sometimes eat lunch. **4.** Anna, Rachelle's dad and <u>I</u> are thinking that you and she are getting warm, but you could get even warmer next to this! **5.** We puzzle-makers thought it might be time for you and her to take a rest in the shade of a <u>b</u>ig tree. **6.** Mom and I put a box in the car; now if you and she will go and gra<u>b</u> it, you'll find that it's a little _____.
Treasure: rabbit

Page 25, Maze
1. Can we and the others... **2.** My idea is... **3.** Both Min and he...
4. If you and they... **5.** Corey and they... **6.** On Friday the Jacksons...
7. My father and I... **8.** Has Leif or he... **9.** He and I... **10.** After Jorge and we... **11.** Greta and he...

Name_____ Date _____

Treasure Hunt

Rachelle's parents have a surprise for her: a new pet! Help Rachelle and her friend Anna through the special treasure hunt and discover what kind of pet awaits her.

Directions: Locate all of the sentences below that use personal pronouns correctly. Make a list of the underlined letters from *only* the correct clues as you do the hunt. When you have finished, rearrange the letters into the name of the new pet. Answer: _____

> **Begin here by choosing one of the two sentence clues.**
> **Follow the correct one to solve the puzzle.**

> Dad and me have hi<u>d</u>den the second clue where birds bathe.

> Rachelle, if you and she look where Dad and I grow vegetables, you will find <u>a</u>nother clue.

Find the place where us parents enjoy a nap <u>o</u>nce in a while after working hard.

If <u>y</u>ou and her have come this far, it's time for you . . . to start over!

Mom and I put a box in the car; now if you and she will go and gra<u>b</u> it, you'll find that it's a little _____.

Go to <u>t</u>he place where the neighbors and we share a gate.

Mom and me hope that you and her are not <u>g</u>etting too tired and have to lie down here!

Anna, Rachelle's dad and <u>I</u> are thinking that you and she are getting warm, but you could get even warmer next to this!

It's up to you and her to find the <u>r</u>ight clue where you and I sometimes eat lunch.

We puzzle-makers thought it might be time for you and her to take a rest in the shade of a <u>b</u>ig tree.

If the clues made up by <u>we</u> parents are not too hard, you should go for a swing.

Punctuation Puzzles & Mazes • Scholastic Professional Books

Pronoun Case

Maze

Name_____ Date _____

Directions: Find the path through the maze by passing only through areas that have sentences in which every personal pronoun is used correctly. The path to the finish will take you through 11 correct sentences. Be careful! There are false paths and lines that block paths.

START

Can we and the others ride with Kira and them?

My idea is for Jen and me to go before Ari and her.

Both Min and he are planning to write to Hal and her.

Mike and me want to play, but we can wait till later.

We students are too young to vote, but Jason and he can.

Give we girls the map and we'll meet him and Di there.

If you and they want to help, take this wrench to Sue and her.

Anita and me sent a card to Ernesto and and them.

Has Leif or he decided about traveling with the girls and us?

One of us hikers has to carry the bag for Mr. Chang and she.

Are Khalil and them ready with their math project?

He and I went to the movies with Mona, Jenna, and her.

Corey and they love to start arguments with Trini and her.

After Jorge and we finish, you and they can use our table.

The jazz concert was a surprise for we girls in the chorus.

My father and I signed up for a pottery class given by Lo and her.

On Friday the Jacksons and we are going to the beach.

Greta and he were so happy to get a call from Tia and him.

FINISH

Unit 5: Unnecessary Tense Shifts

This unit, the first of five devoted to verbs, focuses on helping young writers understand verb tenses so that they won't make unnecessary (and confusing) shifts, beginning a story in the past tense, for instance, but later shifting into the present.

Rule: When you write, establish a verb tense and stick with it (unless there's a good reason to change).

Example: We traveled for two hours on the train, then had to rent a car, and finally *arrive* here six hours later. (correction: *arrived*)

Teaching Tips

★ There are two frequent causes of incorrect tense shifts. First, younger students often don't fully understand what *tense* means and students who have come to English as a second language may not be used to verb tenses like ours. Second, students often hear tense shifts in informal speech: "I walked into the room and who do you think I see standing there?" Furthermore, they may have read stories that change tense from the past to the present in order to make a scene vivid and immediate.

★ The exercises in this unit keep things simple, tackling only relatively obvious shifts from past to present and present to past within a single sentence. (Sophisticated tense problems like the use and misuse of the past perfect are covered in Unit 6.)

Grammar Puzzles & Mazes • Scholastic Professional Books

Mini-Lesson

Students who shift their tenses unnecessarily often have difficulty identifying the tense of verbs. A good way to introduce these exercises is to have a short drill in which you ask your class to name the tense of the verbs that you use, and for this unit you need work only with the past and present tenses.

Simply read sentences aloud—or, even better, fit them together into a short story—and then call on students, asking them to identify the tense of the verb (or verbs) in the sentences. Alternatively, you can develop silent signals, like thumbs up for present-tense verbs and thumbs down for past-tense verbs. Students can demonstrate their understanding by giving the appropriate signal. Although this seems like an elementary drill, you may be surprised at how many of your students will need to think hard in order to identify the tenses correctly.

Answers

Page 28, Word Find
1. takes = took **2.** distributes = distributed **3.** grabbed = grabs
4. brushed = brushes **5.** snatches = snatched **6.** begin = began
7. spotted = spots **8.** started = starts **9.** concludes = concluded

```
D E E G R S S A T R S
R I L J T D E D E E N
T R S A S E H S U R A
E O R T I P S K E P T
N T O I R O U A R U C
S S R K W I R Y U P H
B O P N I P B A S Q E
F E C O N C L U D E D
S P G G T A E S T R T
N G R A B S V I S E O
A L Y M N R E D A E D
```

Page 29, Maze
The correct path goes through: 1. First I try... **2.** In the story...
3. Cindy made... **4.** Maria climbed... **5.** First Sheila... **6.** We tested...
7. The water looks... **8.** When I lost... **9.** When the slides...
10. Santo played... **11.** When the day...
Bonus: There are 13 correct sentences in all. **Also: 12.** The playground... **13.** Darcy played...

Unnecessary Tense Shifts

Word Find

Name_____ **Date** _____

Directions: In each sentence, correct one verb to make the tense—past or present—consistent throughout the sentence. Circle the error and write your correction on the line following the sentence. Check yourself by finding your answers in the grid. (Answers run left, right, up, down, and diagonally.)

D	E	E	G	R	S	S	A	T	R	S
R	I	L	J	T	D	E	D	E	E	N
T	R	S	A	S	E	H	S	U	R	A
E	O	R	T	I	P	S	K	E	P	T
N	T	O	I	R	O	U	A	R	U	C
S	S	R	K	W	I	R	Y	U	P	H
B	O	P	N	I	P	B	A	S	Q	E
F	E	C	O	N	C	L	U	D	E	D
S	P	G	G	T	A	E	S	T	R	T
N	G	R	A	B	S	V	I	S	E	O
A	L	Y	M	N	R	E	D	A	E	D

Example: Theo seals the envelope, puts on a stamp, and then rushed to the mailbox to mail the letter.

___rushes___

1. Jenelle walked into the room, saw the teacher, and then quickly takes her seat.

   _____

2. Mr. Tyler took a huge stack of tests out of the cabinet, smiled wickedly, and then distributes them to the startled class. _____

3. The dog in the movie rushes into the room, barks wildly, and then grabbed his master by the seat of the pants. _____

4. Usually Cindy brushed her hair vigorously, pulls it back into a ponytail, and ties it with a red ribbon. _____

5. After Vashti snatches the ball, she dribbled around three players and sank a lay-up.

   _____

6. My first reaction was a big yawn, but then they sang that wonderful Mexican song and I really begin to like the show. _____

7. In the story, the detective slips silently through the doorway, carefully searches the entire room, but never spotted the necklace hanging on the Christmas tree. _____

8. Whenever Colette sees a bug, she shrieks and then usually started laughing at herself. _____

9. The trip to Yellowstone, which took two days but seemed more like two weeks, concludes with an unforgettable experience. _____

Grammar Puzzles & Mazes • Scholastic Professional Books

Name_____ Date_____

Maze

Directions: Help Paulo find his little sister Tricia at the other side of the playground. Trace a route through 11 sentences that have no unnecessary shifts in verb tense.

★ **Bonus:** How many correct sentences are there in the entire maze? ____

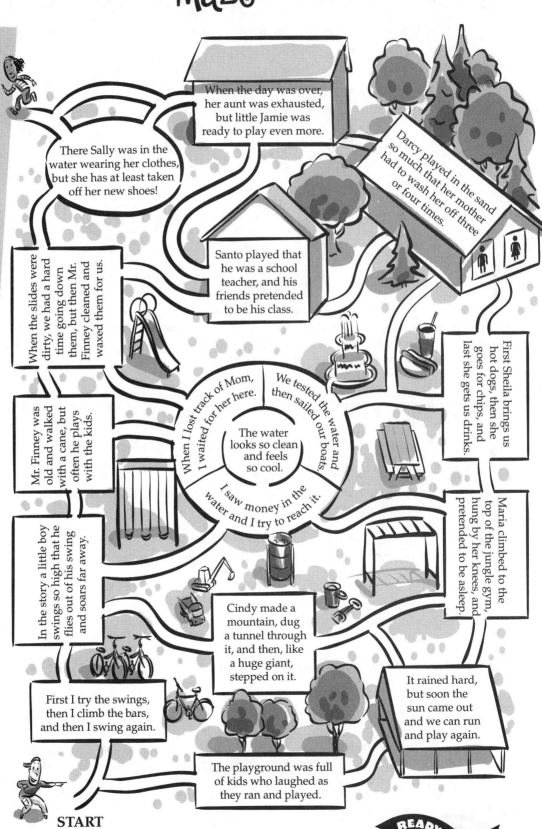

When the day was over, her aunt was exhausted, but little Jamie was ready to play even more.

There Sally was in the water wearing her clothes, but she has at least taken off her new shoes!

Darcy played in the sand so much that her mother had to wash her off three or four times.

When the slides were dirty, we had a hard time going down them, but then Mr. Finney cleaned and waxed them for us.

Santo played that he was a school teacher, and his friends pretended to be his class.

First Sheila brings us hot dogs, then she goes for chips, and last she gets us drinks.

Mr. Finney was old and walked with a cane, but often he plays with the kids.

When I lost track of Mom, I waited for her here.

We tested the water and then sailed our boats.

The water looks so clean and feels so cool.

I saw money in the water and I try to reach it.

Maria climbed to the top of the jungle gym, hung by her knees, and pretended to be asleep.

In the story a little boy swings so high that he flies out of his swing and soars far away.

Cindy made a mountain, dug a tunnel through it, and then, like a huge giant, stepped on it.

It rained hard, but soon the sun came out and we can run and play again.

First I try the swings, then I climb the bars, and then I swing again.

The playground was full of kids who laughed as they ran and played.

START

Unit 6: The Perfect Tenses: Past and Future

By the time I was a fledgling, I already learned three foreign bird songs.

If I were you, I'd learn the past perfect tense of this one.

Both exercises in this unit address problems using the past perfect and future perfect tenses. These are relatively sophisticated verb problems but ones that young writers can master once they understand the situations in which the problems arise.

Definition: A verb's *tense* indicates time in the past, present, or future.

In English besides the simple past, present, and future tenses, we have three more past tenses—*past perfect*, *present perfect*, and *future perfect*. These forms are made up of some form of the verb *have* (used as an auxiliary verb) plus the past participle of the main verb or of the verb *be*: for example, *have driven* (present perfect), *had ridden* (past perfect), *will have seen* (future perfect), *have been driving* (present perfect progressive).

The perfect tenses are commonly used to help us understand that one action occurred prior to another (*I had fixed dinner before she arrived*) or that an action that began before is ongoing (*I have been sneezing all day*).

This unit is devoted exclusively to problems involving the past perfect and future perfect tenses, since these tend to cause the most problems for students.

Rule 1: Use the *past perfect* tense to indicate the earlier of two past actions.

Examples: Standard: She **had** *left* before I made the announcement.

Nonstandard: She *left* before I made the announcement.
(The nonstandard sentence illustrates a common student error: using the past tense for the earlier of two past actions.)

Grammar Puzzles & Mazes • Scholastic Professional Books

Rule 2: Use the *future perfect* tense to indicate an action that occurs before or leads up to another action in the future.

> **Examples: Standard:** By the last leg of the race, I **will have** *run* a distance of five miles.
>
> **Nonstandard:** By the last leg of the race, I *will run* a distance of five miles. (Students sometimes mistakenly use the future tense instead of the future perfect, as in the nonstandard example above.)

Teaching Tip

★ Like many usage errors, those involving the misuse of the past tense for the past perfect tense usually occur because students don't hear the forms used correctly in informal speech. Also, because speakers so often contract the auxiliary verb *had* when using the past perfect, we can miss hearing it when the tense is used correctly. It is very easy, for example, to miss the *'d* of *he'd* in sentences like *If he'd said that earlier, I would have forgiven him.*

Mini-Lesson

Oral practice can be very useful for teaching the perfect tenses. Make the drill fun by creating a compelling situation—a surprise party, for example—and have students make up their own sentences in which they use the past perfect or future perfect correctly to describe something about this situation. Then have them read their sentences aloud and ask their peers to identify the verb that is in the perfect tense. Alternatively, make up sentences yourself, winding them into a little tale to sustain interest.

Answers

Page 32, Elephant Joke
Corrected sentences: 1. ...I had seen... **2.** Correct **3.** ...after she had made... **4.** ...we will have found... **5.** ...he had asked... **6.** Correct **7.** Correct **8.** ...he had gone... **9.** ...he had made... **10.** ...had already left... **11.** Correct **12.** ...will have been married... **13.** ...had already been sold.
Punch line: a sandwich

Page 33, Maze
The path to the finish goes through: 1. When we bought... **2.** By next week... **3.** I had already cared... **4.** If I were you... **5.** If she'd... **6.** On Monday... **7.** Had he had... **8.** I wish he... **9.** If I had known... **10.** By then I hope... **11.** I had seen...

The Perfect Tenses: Past and Future

Name_____ **Date** _____

Elephant Joke

A man riding on an elephant came up to a turnpike tollbooth. The attendant took one surprised look and said, "You must be crazy. You can't ride that elephant out on the turnpike. Don't you see that sign over there: NO RIDING HORSES, MULES, OR OTHER ANIMALS?"

After a short argument, the man turned the elephant around and rode away. Only minutes later the man rode up again, but this time the elephant had a piece of bread tied to his trunk and another piece of bread tied to his tail.

"Didn't I tell you that you can't take that elephant out on the turnpike?" shouted the attendant.

"It's not an elephant," said the man, "It's $\underset{1}{\underline{a}}$ $\underset{2}{\underline{}}\,\underset{3}{\underline{}}\,\underset{4}{\underline{}}\,\underset{5}{\underline{}}\,\underset{6}{\underline{}}\,\underset{7}{\underline{}}\,\underset{8}{\underline{}}\,\underset{9}{\underline{}}$."

Directions: To complete the punch line of the joke, find all of the sentences in the exercise below that don't use the past perfect or future perfect tenses when they should. Using *only* the error sentences, copy the underlined letter into the space in the punch line that has the matching number. The first example has been done for you.

1. I told her I didn't want to see the film because I s*a*w it twice before.   *had seen* (above "s**a**w", marked **1**)

2. At the end of this year Sara will have take**n** four years of Chinese.   **5**

3. Lucia had to can**c**el the trip after she made all the arrangements for it.   **8**

4. By then I hope we will find new **d**rugs to combat such a serious disease.   **5**

5. If he asked me, I would h**a**ve been glad to help.   **3**

6. Although Kenny had b**e**en hurt in an earlier game, he still played in the finals.   **9**

7. When she turns eighteen, she will al**r**eady have been in college for a whole year.   **2**

8. He would have done better in high school **i**f he went to my grade school.   **7**

9. The minute he handed in his te**s**t he realized that he made a mistake on the last problem.   **2**

10. Mic**h**ele already left long before you arrived at the party.   **9**

11. Nora thought that the teacher had given her too little ti**m**e for the essay.   **4**

12. On Sunday my parents **w**ill be married for twenty years.   **6**

13. When my mother fi**n**ally took me to the store, all the good shoes were already sold.   **4**

Grammar Puzzles & Mazes • Scholastic Professional Books

READY-TO-GO REPRODUCIBLES

The Perfect Tenses: Past and Future

Name _____

Date _____

Maze

Directions: Find the path from start (**S**) to finish (**F**) by passing only through areas that have sentences in which the past and future perfect tenses have been used correctly. Spaces with incorrect usage are like blocks and may not be crossed. The shortest path to the finish will take you through 11 correct sentences.

F

I wish he was here.

I had seen his cat once before.

By then I hope I'll have found her.

If I had known you were out, I'd have fed her.

When we looked, we found she went out.

I wish he were thinner.

On Monday she will have been missing two days!

Had he had cats before getting her?

I already played an hour, but he wanted to play more.

She meows as if she was sick.

If she'd seen you, she would have purred.

If I were you, I'd trim his claws.

I wish I was old enough to have my own cat.

By then he came down from the tree.

I had already cared for five cats by age eleven.

By next week she will have weaned her kittens.

Before we saw him, he already saw us and meowed.

If my cat was any bigger, he would catch dogs!

In May he will have had his cat Stripes for twelve years.

When we bought our cat, she had already had her shots.

S

Unit 7: Active and Passive Voice

The exercises in this unit give students practice recognizing the active and passive voice and an understanding of the way verbs allow subtle changes in meaning.

Definition: Verbs in the *active voice* show that the subject of a sentence is doing the action: *The factory* polluted *the river*.

Definition: Verbs in the *passive voice* show that the action is being done to the subject: *The river* has been polluted.

As you can see, the passive voice is handy when we want to avoid responsibility, and it's also useful if we really can't name the person or thing that performed the action: *The car* was stolen *in the night*.

Rule 1: In the active voice the *subject* is the agent that performs the action and the **direct object** (if there is one) receives the action:

> **Example:** The *tornado* destroyed the **house**.

Rule 2: In the passive voice the *subject* receives or is the result of the action of the verb. If there is an **acting agent**, it will appear in a prepositional phrase, usually beginning with the word *by*.

> **Examples:** The *house* was destroyed by the **tornado**.
>
> or
>
> The *house* was destroyed.

Grammar Puzzles & Mazes • Scholastic Professional Books

Teaching Tip

☀ Notice that in the last example, the acting agent is not mentioned. As was indicated above, this is a frequent reason for our choosing to use the passive voice—to avoid having to assign responsibility. Most good writers, however, use the passive voice sparingly because it is usually less forceful than the active voice and can lead to awkward phrasing: *Yesterday a new car was purchased by us.*

Mini-Lesson

Help students see the difference between the active and the passive voices by providing them with practice sentences that can be converted easily from active to passive or vice versa. Then have students convert the example sentences in writing. After some practice, students will be able to switch between active and passive smoothly, but at first most students need to see the sentences written out, either on the board or on a practice sheet.

Examples:

Our newspaper is delivered by a retired postman.

Carol discovered a rare plant.

A talented artist painted that mural.

They were given a free meal by the restaurateur.

Answers

Page 36, Maze
The correct path goes through: 1. This store always... **2.** Thirty years ago... **3.** One of my teachers... **4.** My grandmother still... **5.** My sister often... **6.** Some perfumes... **7.** This author also... **8.** The game... **9.** Someone spilled... **10.** My dog ruined... **11.** My mother inherited... **12.** My grandmother lost... **13.** Jean's mother bought... **14.** Lily makes... **15.** Do they sell...

Page 37, Discover the Author
1. passive **2.** active **3.** active **4.** passive **5.** passive **6.** active **7.** passive **8.** passive **9.** active **10.** active **11.** passive **12.** active
Answer: Toni Morrison

Active and Passive Voice

Name_____ **Date**_____

Maze

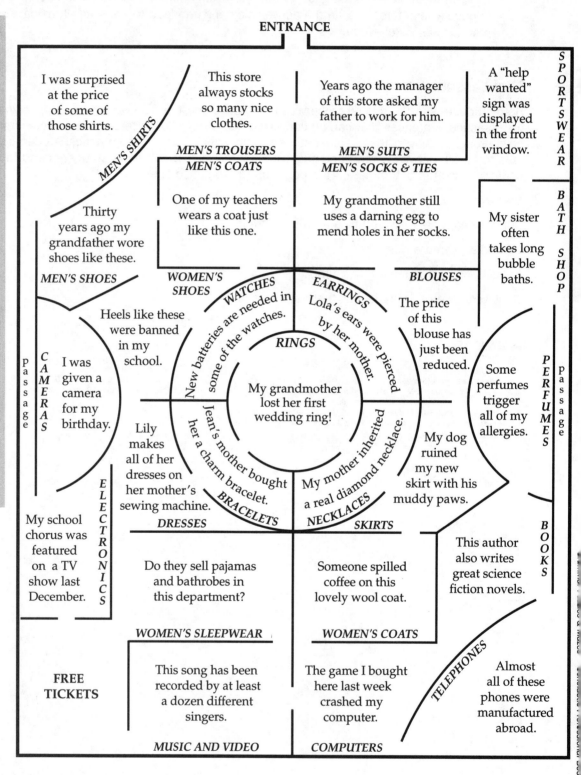

ENTRANCE

I was surprised at the price of some of those shirts.

This store always stocks so many nice clothes.

Years ago the manager of this store asked my father to work for him.

A "help wanted" sign was displayed in the front window.

SPORTSWEAR

MEN'S SHIRTS

MEN'S TROUSERS

MEN'S COATS

MEN'S SUITS

MEN'S SOCKS & TIES

Thirty years ago my grandfather wore shoes like these.

One of my teachers wears a coat just like this one.

My grandmother still uses a darning egg to mend holes in her socks.

My sister often takes long bubble baths.

BATH SHOP

MEN'S SHOES

WOMEN'S SHOES

WATCHES

EARRINGS

BLOUSES

New batteries are needed in some of the watches.

Lola's ears were pierced by her mother.

The price of this blouse has just been reduced.

Heels like these were banned in my school.

RINGS

Some perfumes trigger all of my allergies.

passage

CAMERAS

I was given a camera for my birthday.

My grandmother lost her first wedding ring!

PERFUMES

passage

Lily makes all of her dresses on her mother's sewing machine.

Jean's mother bought her a charm bracelet.

My mother inherited a real diamond necklace.

My dog ruined my new skirt with his muddy paws.

BRACELETS

NECKLACES

DRESSES

SKIRTS

ELECTRONICS

My school chorus was featured on a TV show last December.

Do they sell pajamas and bathrobes in this department?

Someone spilled coffee on this lovely wool coat.

This author also writes great science fiction novels.

BOOKS

WOMEN'S SLEEPWEAR

WOMEN'S COATS

FREE TICKETS

This song has been recorded by at least a dozen different singers.

The game I bought here last week crashed my computer.

TELEPHONES

Almost all of these phones were manufactured abroad.

MUSIC AND VIDEO

COMPUTERS

READY-TO-GO REPRODUCIBLES

Name_____   Date _____

Discover the Author

Which American author won the 1993 Nobel Prize for Literature?

Directions: Find out which author won that famous prize by finishing the exercise below. Determine the tense of each sentence. Circle *Act.* for *active voice* and *Pass.* for *passive voice*. Write the letter that's paired with the correct voice form into the answer spaces. Fill the spaces left to right, starting at the beginning of the "Active" and the "Passive" sections. The first example has been done for you.

1. This book (was given) to me by Jean Marie, my great aunt. (Act.-B; (Pass.-R))

2. Jerry found a wallet on the ground in the park. (Act.-T; Pass.-S)

3. At my school the teachers often wear casual clothes. (Act.-O; Pass.-I)

4. The speech was delivered by a very old but very forceful woman. (Act.-M; Pass.-R)

5. Gold was discovered in California in 1849. (Act.-Y; Pass.-I)

6. Most experts predicted a long, hot summer. (Act.-N; Pass.-L)

7. The mayor was invited to speak at our graduation. (Act.-B; Pass.-S)

8. Mike and Alejandro have been chosen team co-captains. (Act.-R; Pass.-O)

9. The jeweler repaired and cleaned my old watch. (Act.-I; Pass.-E)

10. Students must carefully follow the rules for fire drills. (Act.-M; Pass.-D)

11. The train was delayed by a blizzard. (Act.-U; Pass.-N)

12. We completed the exercise in less than ten minutes. (Act.-O; Pass.-E)

Answer: __ __ __ __   __ __ r __ __ __ __ __
                    ⌣   ⌣
              Active   Passive

Unit 8: Irregular Verbs:
Choose, Come, Take, Begin

> I've just began to read an English grammar book.

> I think you've chosen very wisely.

The exercises in this unit take on four troublesome irregular verbs: *choose*, *come*, *take*, and *begin*. Common nonstandard usages are listed below; standard forms follow in parentheses.

choose	Principal parts: *choose, chose, (have) chosen*
	He *choose* this one. (*chose*)
	Did she *chose* that? (*choose*)
	They have *choosed* the red one. (*chosen*)
come	Principal parts: *come, came, (have) come*
	He *come* over. (*came*)
	She has *came* here before. (*come*)
take	Principal parts: *take, took, (have) taken*
	Has he *took* his pill? (*taken*)
	They *taken* my hat. (*took* or *have taken*)
begin	Principal parts: *begin, began, (have) begun*
	She *begun* to sing. (*began*)
	I have just *began* a new book. (*begun*)

Grammar Puzzles & Mazes • Scholastic Professional Books

READY-TO-GO REPRODUCIBLES

Mini-Lesson

Irregular verbs are so named because their past forms do not follow consistent patterns. Students must learn the forms of each verb individually, and you can help them by discussing mnemonic devices. These memory aids that we all use can be ingenious or silly, as long as the associations help our brains retain the information.

Students love to create and share mnemonic devices. You might start them off with the verbs in this unit by discussing the problem of remembering how to distinguish between *choose* and *chose*. While they rarely make oral errors with these forms, they often misspell them in writing. Suggest mnemonic devices that stress the way we write the two vowel sounds, perhaps something like these sentences: *I chose the rose. I didn't choose the goose.* Then have them come up with their own personal devices for each verb and share them with their classmates.

Answers

Pages 40–41, What's Wrong Here?
Corrections: Choose: How to Choose a Good Pet (title); Mayor Chooses Not to Run (headline); Have I chosen a good book? (check-out)
Take: I Took My Time (title); Have You Taken All Your Belongings? (sign); I should have taken out more books. (check-out) **Begin:** The Day the War Began (title); Oil Cleanup Has Begun (headline); I've already begun reading this one. (at table) **Come:** A Monster Came to Get Me! (title); This book came in late. (check-out); I've come here every day this week. (near table)

Page 42, Maze
The correct path to the finish goes through: 1. The adventure... **2.** We chose well... **3.** Has someone... **4.** Let's choose... **5.** I just took... **6.** Have you taken... **7.** I just began... **8.** Can't we take... **9.** I've chosen... **10.** I've come up... **11.** We have...began. **12.** Now you choose... **13.** It took... **14.** We've come...far! **15.** Now I've begun... **16.** Is that... **17.** I've taken off... **18.** I've begun... **19.** Have we come... **20.** I've taken my...
Bonus: 23 **Also: 21.** I've taken out... **22.** Look how... **23.** We've come...treasure.

Name_____ **Date** _____

What's Wrong Here?

Directions: If you look closely at the picture of this library, you will find 12 errors in the use of the verbs *choose*, *take*, *begin*, and *come*. When you find an error, write the sentence or phrase with the correct verb form in the spaces below.

Corrections

Choose:

1. _____

2. _____

3. _____

Take:

1. _____

2. _____

3. _____

Begin:

1. _____

2. _____

3. _____

Come:

1. _____

2. _____

3. _____

Grammar Puzzles & Mazes • Scholastic Professional Books

READY-TO-GO REPRODUCIBLES

What's Wrong Here? (continued)

Name_____ **Date** _____

Maze

Directions: Rumor has it that there is treasure somewhere in this old haunted house! To reach the treasure, you must pass only through rooms where the verbs in *italics* (all forms of *begin*, *choose*, *take*, and *come*) have been used correctly. (You may pass freely from floor to floor by using the stairs and ladders.) The shortest path to the end will take you through 20 rooms with correct verb forms.

✷ **Bonus:** How many rooms in the entire house contain correctly used verbs? _____

END

TREASURE

Who would ever *chose* to take a bath in that tub?

I've *begun* to feel we're being watched!

You *choosed* the wrong way again.

Have we *come* to a dead end?

Who has *took* my flashlight?

I've *taken* my last step!

I've *began* feeling a little faint!

We've *come* all this way and there isn't any sign of treasure.

I've *taken* off my coat.

Is that the same bat that *came* through here before?

Now I've *begun* to smell a spicy odor!

We've *come* so far!

It *took* some real courage to come up here!

I don't think I'll *chose* those rickety old stairs.

A huge rat just *come* through that door!

I used to like spiders, but I've *began* to hate them.

Haven't we *came* through this room before?

Now you *choose* if we should go further up!

Look how you've *begun* to sweat!

Have you *taken* any notice of those strange eyes in the wallpaper?

Can't we *take* a rest soon?

I've *chosen* to try that door.

I've *come* up with a plan.

I just *took* a deep breath and *came* on up the stairs!

I just *began* to regret that we *came* here.

I feel that we've *took* a wrong turn.

We have to finish what we *began*.

Let's *choose* someone to go up the stairs first.

You certainly *taken* a long time to get that candle lit!

Have you ever *came* here before?

I think we've *chose* the wrong way to go.

Has someone *come* up with a plan for getting back out of here?

We *chose* well when we decided to bring candles and matches.

The adventure has just *begun*.

I've *taken* out my flashlight and tried to turn it on, but for some reason it won't light up.

START

42

Unit 9: Irregular Verbs: Drink, Sit, Set, Lie, Lay, Rise, Raise

I lay awake at night trying to figure out how to use *lie* and *lay*.

I see, but at least you don't have so much trouble that you lie an egg.

This unit deals with some very difficult irregular verb pairs—*lie* and *lay*, *sit* and *set*, *rise* and *raise*, as well as *drink*. Examples of common nonstandard usages are given below; standard forms follow in parentheses.

drink Principal parts: *drink (drinking), drank, (have) drunk*

He *drunk* the water. (*drank*)
She has *drank* it all. (*drunk*)

lie Principal parts: *lie (lying), lay, (have) lain*

Meaning: rest, stretch out, recline

He *lied down*. (*lay*)
She *laid* down in grass. (*lay*)
I have *laid* here too long. (*lain*)
The dog was *laying* in the road. (*lying*)

lay Principal parts: *lay (laying), laid, (have) laid*

Meaning: set down, put, place

He *lay* it there yesterday. (*laid*)
Lie the book on the table. (*Lay*)

sit Principal parts: *sit (sitting), sat, (have) sat*

Meaning: rest, recline, assume a sitting position

She *set* down. (*sat*)
He was just *setting* there. (*sitting*)

set Principal parts: *set (setting), set, (have) set*

Meaning: put down, place

He *sat* the book on my hat. (*set*)

rise Principal parts: *rise (rising), rose, (have) risen*

Meaning: go up, get up, come up

Have the prices *rose* higher? (*risen*)
The river had *raised* two meters. (*risen*)

raise Principal parts: *raise (raising), raised, (have) raised*

Meaning: force up, lift up, increase

They *rose* the prices. (*raised*)

Grammar Puzzles & Mazes • Scholastic Professional Books

Mini-Lesson

Because the verb pairs in this unit sound similar, people make frequent errors in choosing the standard forms, especially with the perennial problem pair of *lie* and *lay*. It has almost become more common to hear "The dog was *laying* in the shade" than the standard form *lying*. To help students master these pairs, first discuss *transitive* and *intransitive* verbs: Only one verb in each pair is *transitive*, or takes a direct object: *lay, set,* and *raise. Lie, sit,* and *rise* are *intransitive*, or do not take direct objects. If there is an object of the action, their choice must be one of the transitive group.

Examples: I *lay* the **book** on the table. (transitive)

I *lie* on the couch. (intransitive)

Also point out to students that we mix up *lie* and *lay* because the present tense of *lay* is the same as the past tense of *lie*, making it very easy for us to pick the wrong verb. Once students know the meaning of the verbs and the principal parts, have them substitute *put* or *place* for *lay* and *rest* or *recline* for *lie* to learn to distinguish between the verbs.

Problem: The scarf was (lying, laying) on the bureau.
Test: The scarf was *resting* or *placing* on the bureau? It was *resting*.
Answer: The scarf was *lying* on the bureau.

Answers

Page 45, Riddle
1. drank (2-O); (3-B) <u>sat</u>
2. lain (6-R); (1-R) <u>sit</u>
3. lying (4-O); (8-E) <u>lie</u>
4. raised (5-R); (6-T) <u>risen</u>
5. None correct; (7-A) <u>laid</u>, (1-B) <u>risen</u>
6. drunk (7-O)
7. set (8-W); (3-S) <u>risen</u>
8. laid (3-M); (1-N) <u>sat</u>
9. lying (1-T); (8-N) <u>rise</u>
Answer: tomorrow

Page 46, Maze
The correct path goes through: 1. The explorers... **2.** She had lain...
3. We were so thirsty... **4.** Were you and Carlos... **5.** The teacher laid...
6. That morning... **7.** With a long lever... **8.** I found... **9.** Who is sitting...
10. I've drunk... **11.** My cat... **12.** Can you... **13.** I've set the vase...
14. The river rose... **15.** Ron laid... **16.** I've sat here... **17.** It rose more!
Bonus: 19 **Also: 18.** The baby... **19.** Lay the letter...

Name_____ **Date** _____

Riddle

I never was, am always to be;

No one ever saw me, nor ever will,

And yet I am the hope of all,

Who live and breathe on this terrestrial ball.

Answer: __ *O* __ __ __ __ __ __
          1   2   3   4   5   6   7   8

Directions: In the sentences below, find the eight correct forms of the verbs *drink, sit, set, lie, lay, rise,* and *raise* and circle the number-letter pair that follows. Use the number-letter pairs to fill in the answer spaces. Be sure to cross out the errors as you go! The first one has been done for you.

1. First we ~~set~~ *sat* (3-B) down at the picnic table and then we had a huge picnic and drank (2-O) lemonade.

2. Lara had lain (6-R) so long in bed that she could hardly set (1-R) up.

3. When my father tried to lay (8-E) down for a nap in his bed, he found the cat already lying (4-O) beneath the covers.

4. Once the sun had rose (6-T), we raised (5-R) the shade and looked out at the lake.

5. We've lay (7-A) out our sleeping bags in the back of the van since the cost of the hotel room has raised (1-B) so much.

6. Even though I had drunk (7-O) a huge glass of water, I was still thirsty.

7. I had set (8-W) a ruler in the bank to see how much the river had raised (3-S).

8. When she set (1-N) down, she saw that someone had laid (3-M) a note on her desk.

9. A tiny wisp of smoke started to raise (8-N) up from where the match was lying (1-T).

Name _____   Date _____

Maze

Directions: Find your way to the end of this maze by passing through 17 areas in which the verbs in *italics* are in the correct form. Watch out for mistakes that involve only the verbs *drink, sit, set, lie, lay, rise,* and *raise.*

⭐ **Bonus:** How many spaces are there in the entire maze that contain only correct verb forms? _____

The hat was *laying* in the road.

The baby has *drunk* all of his milk.

Has the cost of fuel *raised?*

Ron *laid* his pen on the desk an hour! How long has the pie *laid* there?

The river *rose* over a meter after the storm.

I've *sat* here for more!

It *rose* Jo *sat it* down.

Lay Sara down there.

The pen on the *drunk* this.

Can you *raise* this window?

My cat was *lying* on top of the towels.

I've *drunk* all the soda in the house.

The moon has *rose.*

never

END

I *laid* here.

I *set* up.

He

Old Uncle Will was just *setting* on the big sofa.

I've *set* the vase on the coffee table.

Was it Miguel who *lay* this book on my drawing?

The price of sugar has *raised* again.

Who is *sitting* in my chair?

Lay the letter on my desk.

She had *lain* in bed for a whole day.

We were so thirsty that we each *drank* a liter of water.

Were you and Carlos *sitting* with Jonathon?

With a long lever two workers *raised* the end of the car.

I found my hat *lying* in a mud puddle.

Mars has *rose* over the horizon.

START

The explorers *set* out on a frigid morning.

Wendy's hopes for a good evening were steadily *raising.*

The teacher *laid* her book on the desk and laughed.

That morning the sun had *risen* in a strange blue mist.

He *sat* the statue on the tall pedestal.

Have you *drunk* all of your orange juice?

Unit 10: Using Adjectives and Adverbs

Use adjectives and adverbs careful *ly* .

This unit deals with the proper use of adjectives and adverbs, addressing common nonstandard usage. The first two exercises cover the substitution of adjectives for adverbs (*He sings beautiful*), the misuse of *good* for *well* (*He sings good*), and the use of double comparisons (*She is the most smartest in the class*). The third exercise addresses the misuse of superlatives when comparing only two things: *Paula is the* tallest *of the two* instead of the standard: taller *of the two*.

Rule: Use an adjective to modify (describe, clarify) a noun or pronoun; use an adverb to modify a verb, adjective, or another adverb.

> **Examples:** She wrote *clear* **instructions**.
> (The adjective *clear* modifies the noun **instructions**.)
>
> She **wrote** the instructions *neatly*.
> (The adverb *neatly* modifies the verb **wrote**.)

Teaching Tips

* ☆ It is sometimes not immediately clear which word a modifier is actually modifying. In the following sentence, for example, it would be easy to make an "educated" mistake by using the formal-sounding adverb *clearly* even though the construction calls for the adjective *clear*: *She wrote the instructions clear enough to be understood by all*. (Here, the instructions are what are clear; *instructions* is a noun and is modified by an adjective; in this case, *clear*.)

* ☆ The word *well* can be either an adjective or an adverb, but the word *good* can only be an adjective. It is therefore easy to confuse the two.

   Examples:

   He runs well. (*Well* is used as an adverb modifying the verb *run*.)

   He feels well. (*Well* is used as an adjective modifying the pronoun *he*.)

   He feels good about his work. (*Good* is used correctly as an adjective modifying *he*.)

   He runs good. (*Good* is used incorrectly as an adverb modifying *runs*.)

⭐ In conversation we frequently use the superlative when comparing two things. However, in standard usage the comparative should be used to compare two things and the superlative to compare three or more things.

Informal: I have sneakers and sandals, but I like the sandals *best*.

Standard: ...I like the sandals *better*. (This statement makes clear that I am comparing only the sandals and the sneakers.)

Mini-Lesson

Unless students have a clear understanding of the two types of verbs in English, *action* and *state of being*, they will have trouble choosing between adjectives and adverbs. Especially problematic are sensory verbs—*feel*, *sound*, *taste*, *look*, and *smell*—that can mean either actions or states of being. Compare the sentences: *He looked around* anxiously and *He looked* anxious. To compound the confusion, expressions like *I feel* badly *about that* seem to be gaining acceptance. The standard is: *I feel bad... I feel badly* should mean *My sensory abilities aren't up to par.*

The best way to help students understand and retain these distinctions is to have them write their own correct examples, using each of the above five verbs in two contrasting sentences—one in which an adverb is required and one in which an adjective is required. If you want them to tackle two problems at once, ask them to use words *good* and *well* as their adjectives and adverbs.

Examples:

When I saw her, she looked *happy*.

She looked *happily* towards the audience.

The soup tastes *good*.

Taste the soup *well*.

Answers

Page 49, Word Search
1. carefully **2.** fairly **3.** well **4.** suddenly
5. fastest (delete most) **6.** sour **7.** harder
(delete more) **8.** good **9.** suspiciously
10. enchanting. **11.** swiftly **12.** quickly

Page 50, Maze
The correct path goes through: 1. He flies
well! **2.** Move quietly. **3.** He floats...
4. Small animals... **5.** I felt sad...
6. Some birds... **7.** He must... **8.** His cry...
9. He flies... **10.** I feel... **11.** I'll bet...
12. Go down... **13.** This trail...
14. He moves... **15.** Come here...
16. My pack... **17.** I'd happily return...
18. Yes, I'd... **19.** The trip...
Bonus: 23 **Also: 20.** He looks fierce...
21. Why do eagles... **22.** This trip...
23. My binoculars...

Page 51, Do You Know?
1. well, quickly **2.** kindest (delete most),
sweetly **3.** older **4.** infrequently **5.** better
6. powerfully **7.** well **8.** delicious, better
9. forcefully **10.** gently **11.** happier (delete
more) **12.** harder, carefully
Answer: William H(enry) Harrison

Word Search

Name _____ **Date** _____

Directions: In each of the sentences below find an error in the use of adjectives or adverbs. Correct each sentence by crossing out errors and writing in the correct words above the mistakes. Circle your answers in the word find. (Answers run horizontally, vertically, or diagonally.) The first one has been done for you.

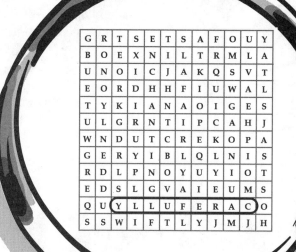

G	R	T	S	E	T	S	A	F	O	U	Y
B	O	E	X	N	I	L	T	R	M	L	A
U	N	O	I	C	J	A	K	Q	S	V	T
E	O	R	D	H	H	F	I	U	W	A	L
T	Y	K	I	A	N	A	O	I	G	E	S
U	L	G	R	N	T	I	P	C	A	H	J
W	N	D	U	T	C	R	E	K	O	P	A
G	E	R	Y	I	B	L	Q	L	N	I	S
R	D	L	P	N	O	Y	U	Y	I	O	T
E	D	S	L	G	V	A	I	E	U	M	S
Q	U	Y	L	L	U	F	E	R	A	C	O
S	S	W	I	F	T	L	Y	J	M	J	H

carefully

1. The teacher asked us to work very ~~careful~~ on our projects.

2. I don't think that he chose the teams fair.

3. Sheila has a strong voice but doesn't hit the notes that good.

4. The storm came up very sudden and drove all of us indoors.

5. Carl's not the most fastest, but he's the best player on the team.

6. This fruit dish tastes sourly to me.

7. Does Danielle work more harder than Eva?

8. I think that Emilio looks really well in that hat.

9. Mr. Hayes was looking suspicious at me.

10. My mother's new perfume smells enchantingly.

11. The deer bounded swift over the open ground.

12. Let's get out of here as quick as possible!

Name_____ **Date** _____

Maze

Directions: Trace a path to the end that goes only through areas with sentences that use adjectives and adverbs correctly. Avoid all sentences with mistakes! The correct route goes through 19 areas containing correct sentences.

★ **Bonus:** How many correct sentences are there in the entire maze? ____

Yes, I'd come here regularly too.

I'd come here happily return here.

Our photos will turn out good.

END

The trip went perfectly!

I'll sleep good tonight!

My pack is starting to feel very heavy.

Don't approach the nest too quick!

Come here slowly!

Pesticides have hurt the eagle populations very bad.

He moves so regally and gracefully that a king would surely be jealous.

Raw meat must taste badly.

He's diving swift towards that meadow!

My binoculars don't adjust very easily.

He doesn't sing good.

This trip is going well!

Go down this path very carefully.

This trail is steep.

He stares cold.

I'll bet his mate is waiting hungrily at the nest.

I feel good about this trip!

He can hear good too.

Talk more quiet.

He flies really fast.

His cry sounds sad.

I felt sad when I saw an eagle sitting unhappily in a cage.

Eagles are much more bigger than I realized.

Why do eagles build their nests so messily?

Small animals below him had better move cautiously!

He must scare other birds badly.

He floats so calmly.

Some birds of prey can be successfully trained by people as hunters.

Move quietly.

He flies well!!

He looks fierce to me.

Eagles soar easy.

START

READY-TO-GO
REPRODUCIBLES

Grammar Puzzles & Mazes • Scholastic Professional Books

Name _____ **Date** _____

Do You Know?

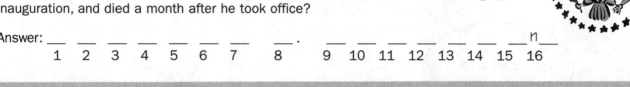

Which president of the United States caught pneumonia, probably at his own lengthy inauguration, and died a month after he took office?

Answer: __ __ __ __ __ __ __   __ .   __ __ __ __ __ __ __n__
        1 2 3 4 5 6 7   8   9 10 11 12 13 14 15 16

Directions: To check the answer to the history question above, find and correct misused adjectives and adverbs in the sentences below. Use the number-letter pairs in parentheses that follow only mistakes to fill in the answer spaces above. The first mistake has been corrected for you.

1. The little girl had been instructed *good* (16-N) [*well*] and looked *carefully* (8-Q) for cars before running *quick* (6-A) across the street.

2. The *most kindest* (2-I) thing she said was that I smiled so *sweet* (14-S).

3. Yvonne was the *oldest* (10-A) of the two, but Danielle seemed more *mature* (12-N).

4. Even though he only practices *infrequent* (8-H), Roberto plays the guitar *well* (9-J).

5. I saw the old Westerns *Shane* and *High Noon recently* (12-T), and I liked *High Noon best* (11-R).

6. Monica got the lifeguard job because she swims *powerful* (4-L) and her stamina is *good* (7-N).

7. Even though I don't sing very *good* (15-O), I appreciate music *immensely* (3-A).

8. Apples and pears both taste *deliciously* (3-L), but I like pears *best* (12-R).

9. Todd, Alex, and Mira all gave speeches, and although Alex's was the *shortest* (9-G), he won the prize because he delivered it so *forceful* (5-I).

10. The breeze made the branches sway *gentle* (7-M) and the leaves rustle *rhythmically* (1-J).

11. Ira seemed *more happier* (13-I) about the team's victory than about having played so *well* (9-G) himself.

12. Of the two, Gus had to work *hardest* (1-W) on the project because Nolan listened to the directions very *careful* (9-H).

Unit 11: Misplaced and Dangling Modifiers

When writing, my modifiers would never dangle!

Misplaced and dangling modifiers are easy to overlook in one's own writing and often in others' writing as well. Because we know what the writer means, we often overlook imprecise sentence constructions. However, precise thinking can be communicated only with precise expression.

Definition: Misplaced modifiers are phrases or clauses that can confuse the reader because they are separated from the part of the sentence that they modify.

Rule 1: It is usually best to put modifiers, especially ones that are adjectives, as close as possible to the words they modify.

Examples: **Misplaced**: He bought a used car for his son that was very rusty.
(His son was not rusty.)

Corrected: He bought his son a used car that was very rusty.

Misplaced: The director decided to do a new ad campaign at our meeting.
(The ad campaign did not happen at the meeting.)

Corrected: The director decided at our meeting to do a new ad campaign.

Grammar Puzzles & Mazes • Scholastic Professional Books

Definition: Dangling modifiers are phrases or clauses in sentences where there is no word that they can clearly or appropriately modify.

Rule 2: There must be a word in the sentence that phrase or clause modifiers can modify appropriately.

Examples:　**Dangling:** Passing a note surreptitiously, her book fell on the floor.
(A book cannot pass a note.)
Corrected: Passing a note, she let her book fall on the floor.
(She passed the note.)

Dangling: When climbing the tree, her grandmother feared little Winnie would fall.
(Grandmother did not climb the tree.)
Corrected: When little Winnie climbed the tree, her grandmother feared she would fall.

Mini-Lesson

When you teach misplaced and dangling modifiers you'll enjoy a chance to hear some very appreciative laughter from your students. Give them several examples of sentences containing both types of style errors (make your examples amusing!), and then ask students to come up with their own examples. After giving them ample time, and perhaps helping those who get stuck, have them read their sentences aloud for correction by their classmates. By creating their own amusing mistakes and sharing them, they'll master the concepts involved.

Sample sentences:

She was wearing a ribbon in her hair that was blue with yellow polka dots. (misplaced)

Her mother bought a toy for her son called Monster Moog. (misplaced)

Braying wildly, the handler tried to calm the angry elephant. (dangling)

Answers

Page 54, Maze
The correct path goes through: 1. Deciding... **2.** Thinking... **3.** The boy... **4.** Not knowing... **5.** Devouring... **6.** The tape... **7.** Having run... **8.** Adoring...
Bonus: 9 **Also: 9.** The insect...

Pages 55–56, Palindromes
All need correcting except numbers 3, 5, 9, 11, and 15.
Answer: "Was it a rat I saw?"

Name _____   Date _____

Maze

Directions: Find a path through the housefly maze from start to finish. You may move only through areas containing sentences in which phrase and clause modifiers have been used clearly. The correct path goes through eight areas containing well-phrased sentences.

✳ **Bonus:** How many well-phrased sentences are in the entire maze? _____

We toured the house with a big porch.

Having run so hard, he was out of breath.

Frightened by the smoke, the fire department was summoned by my neighbor.

The tape that sticks best is in the top drawer.

Devouring his food quickly, he asked for seconds.

The chef told how he cooked for the army in our class.

Clucking loudly, I knew the hen was in trouble.

Adoring his cat, he even walks it.

He asked for clothes for the fire victims if they are clean.

Thinking the play was over, he clapped too soon.

The boy who found your pen was so nice to go looking for you.

Having just been roped, Bret was careful around the pony.

While still in diapers, her father gave her a dictionary.

He gave a toy to his son that needed batteries.

Not knowing if she was right, Ariel turned east.

Deciding the time was nasty, I set out on my trip.

He had a stain on his shirt that was right.

Being so slippery, my aunt avoided the walk.

After giggling in class, our teacher made us stay late.

The insect that intrigues me most is the praying mantis.

Going through the low door, his hat was knocked off.

START

FINISH

READY-TO-GO REPRODUCIBLES

54

Name_____   **Date** _____

Palindromes

Palindromes are words, phrases, and sentences that read the same forward and backward, like *radar*, *kayak*, *Hannah*, and *Madam, I'm Adam*. What palindrome might be overheard in a scary house?

Palindrome: "__ __ __ __ __ $\frac{a}{6}$ __ __ __ __ __ __ __ ?"
        1 2 3   4 5   6   7 8 9   10   11 12 13

Directions: Determine which sentences contain misplaced or dangling modifiers and rewrite any sentence that needs to be corrected. Write the letter found at the end of each sentence with a mistake into the space in the palindrome with the matching number. Do not use letters that follow correct sentences! The first one has been done for you.

1. The hat perched jauntily atop his head that was two feet tall and cone-shaped. (6-A)
The hat, which was two feet tall and cone-shaped, perched jauntily atop his head.

2. Squawking and cackling, the cat was attacked by the angry chicken. (12-A)
_____

3. Deciding that she'd had enough, Olga stalked out of the gory movie. (9-R)
_____

4. Mr. Smith bought a computer for his son that didn't work. (2-A)
_____

5. The house on the corner of the street has a cupola that has always intrigued me. (5-S)
_____

6. The candidate gave a speech in the new school auditorium that he hoped was not too boring. (8-A)
_____
_____

7. Bruised and mushy, the shopper replaced the apples in the bin. (10-I)
_____

8. The mayor decided that the city needed more garbage pick-ups during her lunch break. (3-S)
_____

Name_____ **Date** _____

Palindromes (continued)

9. Having become anxious about the food on the steam table, the chef removed the grilled chicken, which had been sitting out for an hour. (8-A)

_____

_____

10. Having eaten a runny, two-scoop ice cream cone, my shirt was covered with stains. (4-I)

_____

11. After hiking across ten miles of desert, Carlos, who was beginning to think that he had planned poorly, decided to make camp. (1-H)

_____

_____

12. When the pilot became ill, the plane was landed by a passenger without any problems. (11-S)

_____

13. Waking up after a bad dream, his room seemed unfamiliar and threatening. (9-T)

_____

14. Our store policy is to listen patiently to complaints by our customers, no matter how big or small they are. (5-T)

_____

_____

15. Finding a high fence in his path, the deer simply sped up and leapt over it. (7-C)

_____

16. After falling steadily for three days, Barbara wondered if the rain would ever cease. (13-W)

_____

17. Meghan was reading the owner's manual for the new car that she had found in the glove compartment. (1-W)

_____

_____

18. Soaring gracefully over the lake, Darryl was thrilled at sighting an osprey. (7-R)

_____

Grammar Puzzles & Mazes • Scholastic Professional Books

READY-TO-GO
REPRODUCIBLES

Unit 12: Tough Choices: *Like/As, As If, As Though; Fewer/Less, Amount/Number; Among/Between; Beside/Besides*

I feel like I hear the word *like* so often.

Yes, it's as if some people never learned that it's not a conjunction.

This unit covers several groups of words that are often confused and misused.

Like vs. *As, As If,* and *As Though*
Rule 1: *Like*, in standard usage, should introduce a **phrase**—a group of words WITH NO subject and verb. Use *as, as if,* or *as though* to introduce a **clause**—a group of words WITH a subject and verb.

> **Examples:**   **Nonstandard:** He speaks *like* my uncle did.
> **Standard:** He speaks *as* my uncle did.
> **Standard:** He speaks *like* my uncle.
> **Nonstandard:** She looks *like* she is tired.
> **Standard:** She looks *as if* (or *as though*) she is tired.

Fewer vs. *Less; Number* vs. *Amount*
Rule 2: Use *fewer* and *number* before plural nouns or things that can be counted (pencils, people). Use *less* and *amount* before singular nouns that refer to one quantity (air, trouble).

> **Examples:**   **Nonstandard:** I hope we have *less* problems on this test.
> **Standard:** I hope we have *fewer* problems on this test.
> **Standard:** I wish I had *less* trouble finding my seat in the stands.
> **Nonstandard:** A huge *amount* of people were at the stadium.
> **Standard:** A huge *number* of people were at the stadium.
> **Standard:** That's a huge *amount* of work.

Among vs. *Between*

Rule 3: Use *among* with three or more items or when referring to a group. Use *between* for two items or when distinguishing between one item and all the other items in the group.

Examples: **Nonstandard:** Divide the money *between* the three of them.

Standard: Divide the money *among* the three of them.

Standard: Divide the money *between* Paul and the others.

Beside vs. *Besides*

Rule 4: *Beside* means next to; *besides* means in addition to or other than.

Examples: **Nonstandard:** *Beside* my mother, no other family attended.

Standard: *Besides* my mother, no other family attended.

Standard: Sit here *beside* me.

Mini-Lesson

While all of the words listed above are sometimes misused, the most problematic by far is *like*. In fact, it is so often used as a conjunction that this usage may soon become accepted as standard. Students should know, however, that despite the nonstandard use that they see and hear every day, in formal writing *like* still must be used only as a preposition. Time is well spent, then, on oral drills that let students get used to hearing the standard rather than the nonstandard usage. At first, the sentence *He looks as if he's tired* will sound much worse to most of them than *He looks like he's tired*. Spend some time familiarizing your students with the standard usage, either by having them write and share their own sentences using *as*, *as if*, and *as though*, or by making up sentences with blanks where those words should appear and having students supply the correct words out loud.

Answers

Page 59, Do You Know?
1. as if **2.** fewer **3.** beside **4.** among **5.** like **6.** number
7. as though **8.** Besides **9.** number **10.** as if **11.** between **12.** fewer
Number of bones in the hand: 54

Page 60, Maze
The correct path passes through: 1. I feel... **2.** Among the...
3. He talked... **4.** Alissa... **5.** The rabbit... **6.** A large... **7.** Angelo...
8. I asked... **9.** Besides having ... **10.** We divided... **11.** We had...
12. Besides the... **13.** The number... **14.** He looked...
15. Conchita sat... **16.** Joanna... **17.** Among the...

READY-TO-GO REPRODUCIBLES

Name_____ Date _____

Do You Know?

Most of us take our hands for granted, but they are really quite remarkable—and complex!

How many bones are in one human hand? Answer _____

Directions: In each sentence below, choose the answer in the parentheses that will make the sentence correct. Write the number of your choice in the space to the left of the sentence. When you finish, add up the numbers from all the sentences to find the answer to the question above.

____ **1.** He looked at me (like, as if) he had never seen me before!
                          4   6

____ **2.** Matthew was disappointed that there were (fewer, less) people at the game this
                                                        2   5
week than at the last one.

____ **3.** Let's sit down here (beside, besides) the stream.
                          3   1

____ **4.** We had picked ten dozen apples (between, among) the four of us.
                                    2   4

____ **5.** My sister looks (like, as) me but she has a very different personality.
                        1   4

____ **6.** I never remember the (amount, number) of players on a soccer team.
                          3   5

*(**Hint:** If you have identified all the correct answers so far, your subtotal should be 21.)*

____ **7.** The bird acted (like, as though) it had a broken wing.
                      4   5

____ **8.** (Beside, Besides) my parents, there were six others at the party.
        2   6

____ **9.** The (amount, number) of barrels of oil the world uses in a day is staggering.
            1   4

____ **10.** If she had acted (like, as if) she were confident, no one would have known how
                        5   7
nervous she was.

____ **11.** He divided the candy (among, between) Tony and himself.
                          2   4

____ **12.** Liam has (fewer, less) freckles than his brother.
                  7   3

Tough Choices: Like/As, As If, As Though; Fewer/Less, Amount/Number; Among/Between; Beside/Besides

Name_____ Date _____

Maze

Directions: Find your way from start to finish by passing only through areas in which the words in *italics* have been used correctly. Avoid possible mistakes involving the use of *like, as, as if,* and *as though,* as well as *between* and *among, number* and *amount, fewer* and *less,* and *beside* and *besides*. The correct path to the finish passes through 17 areas.

START

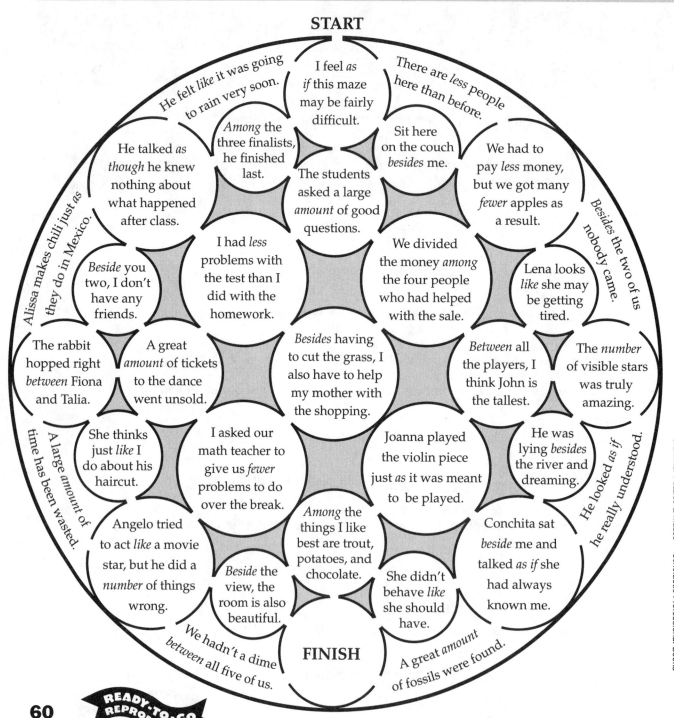

He felt *like* it was going to rain very soon.

I feel *as if* this maze may be fairly difficult.

There are *less* people here than before.

Among the three finalists, he finished last.

Sit here on the couch *besides* me.

He talked *as though* he knew nothing about what happened after class.

We had to pay *less* money, but we got many *fewer* apples as a result.

Alissa makes chili just *as* they do in Mexico.

The students asked a large *amount* of good questions.

Besides the two of us nobody came.

Beside you two, I don't have any friends.

I had *less* problems with the test than I did with the homework.

We divided the money *among* the four people who had helped with the sale.

Lena looks *like* she may be getting tired.

The rabbit hopped right *between* Fiona and Talia.

A great *amount* of tickets to the dance went unsold.

Besides having to cut the grass, I also have to help my mother with the shopping.

Between all the players, I think John is the tallest.

The *number* of visible stars was truly amazing.

A large *amount* of time has been wasted.

She thinks just *like* I do about his haircut.

I asked our math teacher to give us *fewer* problems to do over the break.

Joanna played the violin piece just *as* it was meant to be played.

He was lying *besides* the river and dreaming.

He looked *as if* he really understood.

Angelo tried to act *like* a movie star, but he did a *number* of things wrong.

Among the things I like best are trout, potatoes, and chocolate.

Conchita sat *beside* me and talked *as if* she had always known me.

Beside the view, the room is also beautiful.

She didn't behave *like* she should have.

We hadn't a dime *between* all five of us.

FINISH

A great *amount* of fossils were found.

READY-TO-GO REPRODUCIBLES

Grammar Puzzles & Mazes • Scholastic Professional Books

Unit 13: Usage Review

These mazes review all of the topics covered in this book. The Turkey Maze reviews standard agreement between subjects and verbs and between pronouns and antecedents. The Diamond Maze reviews usage concepts involving verbs—subject and verb agreement, the past and future perfect tenses, and the standard forms of irregular verbs. The Pig Maze reviews agreement of pronouns and antecedents, cases of personal pronouns, adjectives and adverbs, and the frequently misused words *amount, number, fewer, less, beside, besides, between, among, like, as if,* and *as though.*

Answers

Page 62, Turkey Maze
The easy path goes through: 1. Every class...
2. Here's a pig! **3.** Is each... **4.** Does one of
you... **5.** Every animal... **6.** Every ram is...
7. Has every one of... **8.** Neither of these...
9. Each horse... **10.** Most of the geese...
11. Has the silo... **12.** There are...
13. One of... **14.** Not one...
The difficult path goes through: 1. Every
class... **2.** Here's one. **3.** Does each...
4. Is everyone... **5.** Everybody is... **6.** Neither
this... **7.** Each of... **8.** Every tool...
9. Do all... **10.** Where's... **11.** Neither the...
12. Has either... **13.** One of the... **14.** Do any...
15. Here's a... **16.** Neither of...
17. Each of... **18.** Has he... **19.** Where's...
20. Is each... **21.** There is... **22.** Does the
farm... **23.** Every teacher. **24.** Each of...
25. The children... **26.** Either this...
27. Neither Ari... **28.** Has everybody...
29. One of... **30.** Do all... **31.** This farm...
32. One of... **33.** Was it... **34.** Not one...
35. There's... **36.** Neither of... **37.** Each of...
38. One of... **39.** Not one...

Page 63, Diamond Maze
The correct path passes through: 1. Is one...
2. The hen... **3.** The dough... **4.** Anita...
5. Not one of the animals... **6.** When I...
7. Because she'd... **8.** Both Dara... **9.** Neither
Heather... **10.** After Tomas... **11.** Neither of the
girls... **12.** Either Carlos... **13.** Sarah laid...
14. I can't believe... **15.** If he...
16. We could... **17.** Each of them...
18. By Wednesday... **19.** I could...
20. Has anybody... **21.** Neither has chosen...

Page 64, Pig Maze
The correct path goes through: 1. It looks...
2. Each dog... **3.** He and I... **4.** Besides us...
5. Neither Alvin... **6.** He is... **7.** Decide...
8. Get a... **9.** I feel... **10.** We saw...
11. Did each... **12.** Michele... **13.** Andre...
14. No one...
Bonus: She offered it to Stu and me.

Name_____ Date _____

Turkey Maze

Directions: There are two paths to the finish, each starting at (**S**) at the turkey's feet and ending at (**F**) in his bill. Both paths require you to go only through areas that contain sentences in which subjects and verbs agree and pronouns and antecedents agree. The easy path to the finish passes through 14 correct sentences; the difficult path goes through—yes!—39 correct sentences.

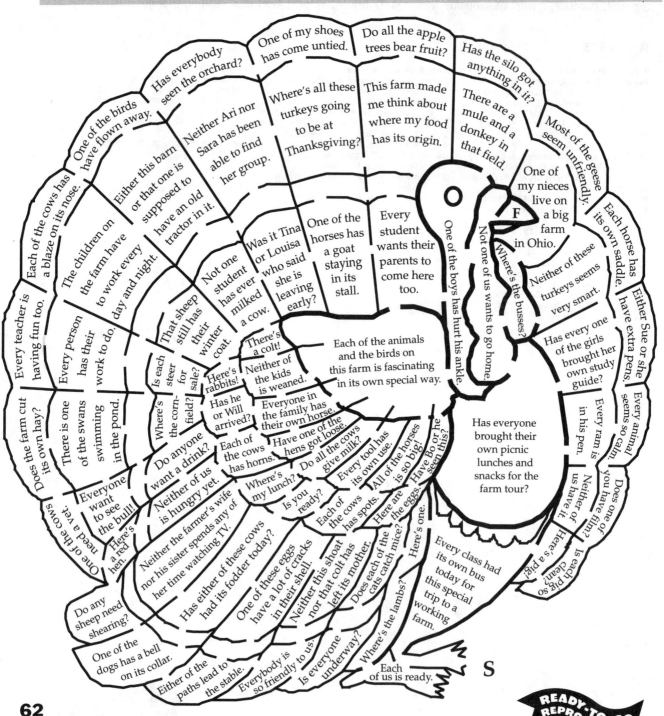

Grammar Puzzles & Mazes • Scholastic Professional Books

Diamond Maze

Name _____ **Date** _____

Directions: This is a review of usage concepts involving verbs—subject and verb agreement, the past and future perfect tenses, and the standard forms of irregular verbs. Avoid areas that contain a nonstandard use of a verb! The correct path to the end passes through 21 areas.

Neither Heather nor Frances has brought enough money for the roller coaster.

Both Dara and Vincente are sitting with the older kids at the show.

Because she'd lain there so long, the coach was worried.

Do either Chris or Geoffrey have a pencil?

The hen has laid a very big egg.

Is one of the ponies quite gentle?

He could have laid down longer.   **START**   I think he choose very poorly.

The dough had risen, but then it fell.

Anita has taken a shower and begun to get dressed.

Not one of the five divers have raised a sunken pirate ship before.

By the time Gregory has begun his homework, I will already be done for an hour.

After Tomas had set the pot on the stove to boil, he chose several fresh herbs to flavor the sauce.

Neither of the girls has laid out artwork before, but both of them have done computer graphics.

Mary thought that we brought all the wrong things for a day on a crowded beach.

We could have gone to a good movie, but then we chose this one.

Each of them was unaware of the deer lying nearby.

I don't think she brang enough food.

Neither has chosen to go.   **END**   Where's your mom and dad?

He had took a wrong turn.

If we had drunk more water before the hike, we could have went even farther.

Her mother came for her after her father already picked her up.

When I get home, Leslie will have been there an hour.

Not one of the animals was lying in shade.

Ted really don't know about it.

By Thursday we will go to five different states and take three more rolls of film.

I can't believe that Quincy has lain in bed for over fourteen hours!

If he had begun sooner, he could have completed it all.

Prince was setting just where we left him.

Has anybody seen my sister?

I could have gone even faster.

By Wednesday she will have chosen a topic.

There was now just a swamp where once a big lake was.

Sarah laid her head down on her desk and began to sniffle and sob.

Either Carlos or Jo has brought some binoculars if you choose to go bird watching.

63

Grammar Puzzles & Mazes • Scholastic Professional Books

Pig Maze

Grammar Puzzles & Mazes • Scholastic Professional Books

Directions: Find your way from the start (**S**) at the pig's nose to the finish (**F**) at its tail by passing only through areas with sentences containing correct agreement of pronouns and antecedents, personal pronouns, adjectives and adverbs, and the words *amount, number, fewer, less, beside, besides, between, among, like, as, as if,* and *as though.* The correct path will take you through 14 areas.

★ **Bonus:** There is one other correct sentence in the maze. Which is it? _____

It looks as if you and I didn't win.

Think quick!

Zach and me will help.

Each dog has its own bowl.

I didn't explain it good.

Mia and I feel very good today.

Between the three of us we had only two dimes.

There are less bugs now.

He and I are sharing.

Work careful!

Min thinks like they do.

Besides us, two more are coming.

I think Shane played bad.

Get a book from Dara or her.

Decide between these two.

He looks like he is angry.

My car has less rust spots.

Sit here besides me and her.

He is the older of the two.

I shook the can vigorous.

I am taller than her.

Neither Alvin nor Sam had brought his uniform.

Andre acted as if he knew her.

Does everyone have their pen?

Gary and me are going today.

Nicky is the fastest of the two.

No one besides me cares.

Less problems arose.

She offered it to Stu and me.

I reacted like I always do.

Speak gentle.

Did each of the girls bring her own supplies?

We saw a large number of farm animals.

The Tylers and us have good seats for the play.

I feel as if I'm getting a bad cold.

Every one of the boys tried their hardest.

Beside me, there is no one who is ready.

The menu seems to offer less choices now.

Michele usually paints just as well as she.

You should give the book to either Rex or he.

S

F

64